A Classical Christmas

Piano Solos by Emily Tufenkjian

Moderate

CONTENTS

Lillenas Publishing Company
Kansas City, MO 64141

O Come, O Come, Emmanuel

In the setting of Chopin's *Prelude in E Minor, Op. 28, No. 4*

Plainsong, adapted by THOMAS HELMORE, 1854
Arr. by Emily Tufenkjian

Christ Was Born on Christmas Day

With Handel's *He Shall Feed His Flock* from The Messiah

Trad. German Carol
Arr. by Emily Tufenkjian

Tenderly ♩ = ca. 120

"He Shall Feed His Flock" (G. F. Handel)

What Child Is This?

In the setting of Rimsky-Korsakov's *Sheherezade*

Trad. English Melody
Arr. by Emily Tufenkjian

ff

accel. poco a poco to the end

Hark! the Herald Angels Sing

In the setting of Tchaikovsky's *Russian Dance* from The Nutcracker Suite

FELIX MENDELSSOHN
Arr. by Emily Tufenkjian

Lively ♩ = ca. 126

March of the Kings

In the setting of J. S. Bach's *Musette*

Traditional French Melody
Arr. by Emily Tufenkjian

Moderate march ♩ = ca. 126

Away in a Manger

In the setting of Brahms' *Lullaby*

JAMES R. MURRAY
Arr. by Emily Tufenkjian

Gently ♩ = ca. 80

O Come, Little Children

In the setting of Humperdink's *Hansel and Gretel*

J. A. P. SCHULZ
Arr. by Emily Tufenkjian

The First Noel

In the setting of J. S. Bach's *Minuet*

From W. Sandys' *Christmas Carols*, 1833
Arr. by Emily Tufenkjian

Moderato ♩ = ca. 100

We Three Kings

In the setting of Mozart's *Symphony #40, in G Minor,* 2nd Movement

JOHN H. HOPKINS, Jr.
Arr. by Emily Tufenkjian

Allegro ♩ = ca. 128

Angels From the Realms of Glory

In the setting of J. S. Bach's *Gavotte*
and Pachelbel's *Canon in D*

HENRY SMART
Arr. by Emily Tufenkjian

Silent Night

In the setting of Beethoven's *Moonlight Sonata*

FRANZ GRÜBER
Arr. by Emily Tufenkjian